DEATH THE GATEWAY TO LIFE

Adapted from the teaching of

GILBERT SHAW

by

SISTER EDNA MONICA SLG

SLG PRESS
Convent of the Incarnation
Fairacres   Oxford
0X4 1TB

Sixth Impression 1985

ISBN 7283 0010 9
ISSN 0307-1405

INTRODUCTION

'Brethren, I would not have you be ignorant concerning them which are asleep; that ye sorrow not, even as others which have no hope' (1 Thess. 3:13).

This understanding of the Christian hope in the resurrection which St. Paul expressed for the early Church is a truth which is all too easily forgotten in our day. Death is one of the 'facts of life' which men tend to refuse to face until it directly confronts them. How contrary this is to St. Paul's protestation, 'I die daily' (1 Cor. 15:31), and his confident affirmation that 'to me to live is Christ and to die is gain' (Phil. 1:21). It is this essentially biblical doctrine which Father Gilbert Shaw, our late Warden, expounded and developed and brought home to us in the detailed living out of our daily lives as Sisters of the Love of God.

The substance of what follows is based largely upon homilies which he gave when one of our Sisters was faced with sudden death; but his words have a universal application, and challenge us so to live in love and dependence on God, and to die to our selfish nature, that we may say with St. Catherine of Siena, 'The love of thy mercy will be my excuse before the face of thy lovingkindness' (*Dialogue*, Ch. XXX).

Sister Edna Monica SLG
Fairacres
1971

The earthly life is not the end of man,
It is the place where man is set
to learn to love both God and man,
to witness, to endure, to live and die
for love of God and man.

The Face of Love, Gilbert Shaw

Dependence

'I trusted in thee, O Lord: I said, thou art my God, my times are in thy hand' (Ps. 31:14,15). These words express the absolute simplicity of our dependence on God which we learn through humbly seeing all people, things and circumstances as having their source and their completion in him. Everything has being because being comes from God, and there is no being which is not for God and to be given back to God, In order to understand this we need to submit our intellect, emotions and will to Christ and allow them to be drawn into a unity in him of willing the will of God. Our times are in his hand; all the circumstances of our lives, health and sickness, everything; for all that belongs to us belongs to God. 'Naked came I out of my mother's womb, and naked shall I return thither: the Lord gave and the Lord hath taken away; blessed be the name of the Lord' (Job 1:21).

We cannot know the time or manner of any person's death, but we can believe that it comes within the scope of God's will for his or her fulfilment. To desire nothing but God's will is to be in God's timing so that we are entirely dependent on him for all things. Christ's manhood was gathered up into the victory of the Resurrection through the perfection of his surrender to the Father's will. 'All things are possible unto thee: take away this cup from me: nevertheless not what I will, but what thou wilt' (Mark 14:36). Our human life is gathered into Christ's humanity, and the purpose of Christian discipline is that there may be no obstacle left in us to hinder our surrender to him, so that we may be an open channel through which his love may flow unimpeded.

In the face of death both our love and our surrender meet their final testing on earth. It is only if we have built up the habit of giving our will to

1

be one with God's will throughout our life that we shall be able to meet our death simply, as just another opportunity to say a loving 'Yes' to God and so to complete our willing surrender to him. If this is our disposition we can accept his will peacefully and wait patiently until pain and suffering are ended and we are taken through death into eternal life.

Continuity

The wonder of death is that in it our earthly life is brought to completion and all our aspirations are fulfilled. 'When thou saidst, Seek ye my face; my heart said unto thee, Thy face, Lord, will I seek' (Ps. 27:8). When time in the earthly sense ceases and there is only the wonder of eternity before us we shall be confronted with the vision we have always desired and we shall have the fruit of our seeking. 'His servants shall serve him; and they shall see his face' (Rev. 22:3,4). In fact the whole of this life is ours in order that there should be such a giving of self that, when death comes, there is nothing in us to hide the face of Love. One aspect of the mystery of death which is often missed is this aspect of continuity. Death is not an end. In one sense it is a beginning, but far more, it is continuity; the taking onward into eternity of all that we have done and are and will be.

We so easily forget that the Church does not consist only of those of us who are alive on earth but also of those who are alive beyond the grave. St. Paul says that here and now we are already 'fellow-citizens with the saints, and of the household of God' (Eph. 2:19), and that we are gradually being built up into the Heavenly City, the New Jerusalem, 'which is the Mother of us all' (Gal. 4:26). We, in this world, are fellow-citizens with those who have gone before us. There is continuity. We are fellow-citizens with the saints; that is, those who are filled with God.

This continuity is a first-fruit of our one life in Christ which we share with the saints. Our Lord in his divine compassion takes the whole of humanity from the first Adam to the last man into his own sanctification and therefore he can say, 'for their sakes I sanctify myself' (John 17:19). Christ's life of sanctification goes through the whole of time and embraces the whole of space; it goes into the unity of the heavenly city and draws everything to be fully responsive to God in eternity. By him we are created and are able to respond freely in Christ because we have been given the Spirit. St. Paul speaks of our receiving the image of Christ when he says, 'We all, with open face, beholding as in a glass the glory of the Lord, are changed into the same image, from glory to glory, even as by the Spirit of the Lord' (2 Cor. 3:18).

2

Because our life is incorporated into Christ, death cannot bring that life to an end for already our life is 'hid with Christ in God' (Col. 3:3), and 'when Christ who is our life shall appear then shall we also appear with him in glory' (Col. 3:4).

We must hold fast to this continuity which we affirm in the Creed in the words, 'I look for the resurrection of the dead'. In saying these words we assert our faith in the continuity of body, soul and spirit and that we are one unity, created for one purpose; to be all for God. Therefore we who, as Christians, are called to witness to this purpose and by the dedication of our lives to bring in eternal life, are not deprived by their calling home at the close of the earthly pilgrimage of any one of those who are with us in that pilgrimage.

Human death is a door through which all that we are as a person is taken on for judgment and for perfection. ' "Happy are the dead who die in the faith of Christ! Henceforth", says the Spirit, "they may rest from their labours; for they take with them the record of their deeds" ' (Rev. 14:13). The 'record of their deeds' is the whole being of the person which has been built up in the eartly life and this is taken through death into eternity.

However, a door not only connects, it also separates. This means that there is, of necessity, a real separation in death which is as real as the aspect of continuity, and we should endeavour to hold the two realities in balance. In time we can think of the separation of the body and soul because the body of matter belongs to space and, therefore, as we bury the body, we say at the graveside, '...earth to earth, ashes to ashes, dust to dust...' The body returns again to the dust from which it was formed; but the soul with all its memory, with all that it has become through the life on earth, through its capacity of spirit that enables us to perceive and live for God, takes with it all that we are, all that we have built into our conscious being and our unconscious being, which together forms our completeness as a person.

Joy and confidence in death

Nevertheless, ideally, there is great joy in the passing of those who love God. Here then is the vital importance of submitting all the levels of our natural life to God for transformation, for what is only suppressed into our unconscious, will come out and assert itself as our bodily strength fails and the control of our will weakens. It is sometimes his unconscious suppressed pride which makes a man cling so hard to his right to life. As long as we can serve God according to his will it is right to fight for life; but when God calls,

3

it must be our joy to give ourselves in the same way that Christ himself commended his soul into the hands of the Father (Luke 23:46).

The Christian is aware that 'here we have no permanent home, but we are seekers after the city which is to come' (Heb. 13:14). It is evident in all the New Testament epistles that our life on earth is but a prelude to a fuller life which is reached by passing through death. Death is but a passage, There is an element of terror in the passage of death, a terror vividly realised by the pagan who fears death as an end or a loss of all he knows and a going into the great unknown. To us as Christians, in one sense it is not a going into an unknown. The wonder and the glory is unknown because we have not experienced it. Nevertheless we have confidence that death will be for us a passage into an entirely new life. In death we pass from the life of pilgrimage and enter upon our full inheritance as citizens in the Kingdom of God, and as 'we have worn the likeness of the man made of dust' so, having passed through death, 'we shall wear the likeness of the heavenly man' (1 Cor. 15:49).

Death as witness of eternity

The Epistles to the Hebrews gives us yet another way of looking at death for it emphasises that death is essentially an act of witness to our faith in God. The Epistle exhorts us to 'run with patience the race that is set before us, looking unto Jesus the author and finisher of our faith', and lest we become wearied, we are reminded that we 'have not yet resisted unto blood, striving against sin' (Heb. 12:1ff). In the same chapter mention is made of the 'cloud of witnesses', the saints who have gone before and who encourage us and with whom, as we have seen, we are already fellow-citizens.

So in death there is the place of the martyrs, those who give up their lives as the witnesses of eternity and of a total response to God, There is too the place of what we may call 'white martyrdom', that is, the witness of those who while not called to die bodily for their faith, yet bear witness in their lives by sharing in the Christian conflict. (Cp. 1 Peter 5:8-11). For all faithful bearing with suffering, whether it be of mind or body, is part of the continuity of overcoming that which has fallen short of or rebels against God in creation. 'Here the fortitude of God's people has its place—in keeping God's commands and remaining loyal to Jesus. Moreover I heard a voice from heaven, saying, "Write this: 'Happy are the dead who die in the faith of Christ!' " ' (Rev. 14:12, 13).

4

Three kinds of death

We can distinguish in the Bible three kinds of death. First, there is 'temporal death' which is the separation of the soul and spirit from the body, and of this we may ask with the Psalmist, 'What man can cling to life and not see death?' (Ps. 89:48). Moreover, because man was made for immortality, the cries of Job find a deep echo in our own hearts and we share his lament, 'Man that is born of woman is of few days and full of trouble . . . Man dieth and wasteth away: yea, man giveth up the ghost, and where is he?' (Job 14:1,10)

There is also a 'spiritual death' when both the soul and body of man are separated from God by wilful sin. It is primarily from such spiritual death that Zacharias foresees deliverance in his prophecy of John the Baptist:—

> *You will be the Lord's forerunner, to prepare his way*
> *and lead his people to salvation through knowledge of him,*
> *by the forgiveness of their sins:*
> *for in the tender compassion of our God*
> *the morning sun from heaven will rise upon us,*
> *to shine on those who live in darkness, under the cloud of death.*
> *(Luke 1: 76-79).*

The book of Revelation (chapter 20) speaks of yet another kind of death: 'the second death', which is the perpetual separation of the whole man from God's presence for all eternity. Perhaps twentieth century man does well if he pauses to consider the reality of this possibility: that man by his own choice, or even, perhaps, by his failure to make a definite choice of serving God rather than his own selfish ego, can forfeit the eternal union with God for which he was destined when he was created. If the earthly life has been used only for its own sake, to please the self, then all that remains at death is the continual turning round in the mind and memory of this desire or that desire in the frustration of self which *is* separation from God.

Christ the conqueror of death

The Jews through their growing experience of the nature of God came to realise that there must be a final manifestation of his justice, and in the centuries just before Christ many of them came to believe in the resurrection of the dead. Martha, for example, could affirm of Lazarus, 'I know that he will rise again at the resurrection on the last day'. Only God's own act could antedate the 'last day', and God *has* antedated it. That is the Christian 'Good'

News'. 'I am the resurrection and I am life', said Jesus. 'If a man has faith in me, even though he die, he shall come to life; and no one who is alive and has faith shall ever die' (John 11:24-26).

The physical body is subject to death on account of sin. 'It was through one man that sin entered into the world, and through sin death, and thus death pervaded the whole human race, inasmuch as all men have sinned' (Rom. 5:12). But the physical is not held by death, as our Lord makes absolutely clear and certain. That is the good news proclaimed by the Church. 'For if the wrongdoing of that one man brought death upon so many its effect is vastly exceeded by the grace of the one man, Jesus Christ', and 'those who receive God's grace and his gift of righteousness, live and reign through the one man, Jesus Christ' (Rom. 5:16, 17). Through the divine mercy presented in life we are taken, by God's grace, into Christ's eternal life, which is the firstfruits of the dead. Death had no hold on him. The physical life which Christ took upon himself is transformed in him into the mystery of life through and beyond death. And 'if we have become incorporate with him in a death like his, we shall also be one with him in a resurrection like his' (Rom. 6:5). The triumphant words of the glorified Christ are, 'I am he that liveth, and was dead; and, behold, I am alive for evermore, Amen; and have the keys of hell and death' (Rev. 1:18).

Our saviour Jesus Christ has 'broken the power of death and brought life and immortality to light through the Gospel' (2 Tim. 1:10). 'We see in Jesus one who is now crowned with glory and splendour because he submitted to death', for 'by God's grace he had to experience death for all mankind' (Heb. 2:9). For our sake Jesus underwent temporal death. From his mysterious and awful cry on the cross, 'My God, my God, why has thou forsaken me?' (Mark 14:34) it would seem that in being 'made sin for us' (2 Cor. 5:21) Jesus knew in his own spirit the agony of spiritual death, of being cut off from the life of God. However 'we know that Christ, once raised from the dead, is never to die again: he is no longer under the dominion of death. For in dying as he died, he died to sin, once for all, and in living as he lives, he lives to God' (Rom. 6:9, 10). And 'these are the words of him who was dead and came to life again . . . Only be faithful till death, and I will give you the crown of life. He who is victorious cannot be harmed by the second death' (Rev. 2:8, 10, 11).

Praying for the dead

In this confident faith the Church has from the very earliest times prayed for those who have died, and this prayer has been a work springing not only from faith, but also from a living hope and an unending love. Love can have no end, for 'God is Love' (1 John 4:9). Therefore our love goes on with those who have died as a continual offering, and their love for us also goes on and is transformed as they are gathered up more completely into the knowledge of Christ.

In particular, our prayer for the departed is that their memory should be made completely free, because it is hard to shake off that which is so much a part of ourselves. We pray, 'May they rest in peace'. That peace is the activity of love, the receiving of the being and purpose of God and the returning of it, without any separation of self. Our prayer for the departed is effective in proportion as our own self-emptying allows love to overflow from us. For sanctity is the work of God, an activity of Love, the love of God poured out on and into his creation, to draw out that response of love of which he has made his creatures capable, so that they, receiving and responding through free will, may be made perfect in the purpose of their creation: to love and to be increased in loving.

As St. Augustine so truly said, 'Thou hast made us for thyself and our hearts are restless until they find their rest in thee'. So we pray, 'May they rest in peace', may they enter that rest which is the state in which the purpose of life has been accomplished; may they find rest in him who created them for himself.

Temporal death is but the separation of the soul from the body and does not necessarily bring the soul into a state of rest. If the soul is entangled with, and tied to, the things of time and of this world, it cannot find rest but only frustration and separation and darkness. But death is a thing of wonder if the soul can give itself utterly into God's will and completely leave behind the succession of time with its entenglements. Death is the gate of life if we die to self so that the bodily life can be fulfilled in finding its true purpose of responding to God. Therefore we pray for the departed, that they may see the wonder of the Divine Mercy with unveiled face and that, as they receive the mercy, so they may also accept the judgment.

'Happy are the dead who die in the Lord'.

What a wonderful thing it is to be a Christian! As we are called to lay down our work in this life, we can look confidently to the Divine Harvester to take us into rest, into the perfection of unity where alone is rest, when the will of God is wholly fulfilled in us. Indeed 'happy are the dead who die in the faith of Christ' for they take with them the first-fruits of their purification begun in this life so that they may be harvested in heaven. We enter into the labours of those who have gone before us. They take with them their fruit, and we have to go on labouring in the field which they have cultivated. We carry on their work; we add our service to theirs, and by so doing we are cultivating the Kingdom which is not of this world, but is being harvested out of this world.

> Then a voice came from the throne which said, 'Praise our God, all you his servants, you that fear him, both great and small! . . . The Lord our God, sovereign over all, has entered on his reign! Exult and shout for joy and do him homage, for the wedding-day of the Lamb has come! His bride has made herself ready, and for her dress she has been given fine linen, clean and shining'. (Now the fine linen signifies the righteous deeds of God's people.) (Rev. 19:5-8)

Each one of us has a part in making up some thread in that fine linen which is the adornment of the Bride, in contributing to the glory of the Bride whom Christ will take at the end of all things into the glory of the heavenly city, where there is nothing that makes a lie, nor any distortion, where all the entanglements of man's fallen nature will have been swept away through the soul's giving of the whole self to be purified in the Passion of our blessed Lord. That is the wonder of being a Christian!

In the face of this wonder, we may well ask, as St. Paul does in his second letter to the Corinthians, 'Who is sufficient for these things?' (2 Cor. 2:16). We know that we are not 'sufficient of ourselves but our sufficiency is of God' (3:5), for 'from first to last this has been the work of God' (5:18). Alongside St. Paul's confidence that God is at work in the Christian, is his awareness that our response and cooperation are all-important, for we are 'workers together with God' (6:1), and 'we must all have our lives laid open before the tribunal of Christ, where each must receive what is due to him for his conduct in the body, good or bad' (5:10).

'At eventide they will examine thee in love'

Death is a great mystery, and as we consider what happens to the soul after death we must recognise the limitations of our finite minds in respect to things infinite and beyond our full comprehension and knowledge.

One of the saints who speaks to us most clearly on the subject is St.

Catherine of Genoa. In her *Treatise on Purgatory*, she says that those who have died 'may no longer change the will with which they have passed out of this life, in which passage the soul is made stable in good or evil in accordance with its deliberate will' (ch. IV). She says further that 'the soul goes to the place ordained for it, unguided save by the nature of its sin' (ch. VII).

In this expression there seems to be an echo of the words of St. Paul, who warns us to 'lay aside that old human nature, which is sinking towards death' (Eph. 4:22). In this context, St. Paul is using the term 'human nature' to denote humanity in its sinfulness, as opposed to God. Such opposition inevitably pulls the soul away from God, so that at death the soul, as it were, 'sinks by its own weight', its disposition and choice between God or self having been built up and formed incontrovertibly by its earthly living.

St. John of the Cross would have us remember that 'At eventide they will examine thee in love' (Maxim 57). St. Catherine of Genoa speaks of the effect of this examination in her *Treatise* saying, 'When the soul sees itself drawn by God with such loving fire, then it is melted by the heat of the glowing love for God, its most dear Lord, which it feels overflowing it . . . . It is the sight of these things which begets in the souls the pain they feel in Purgatory' (ch. IX).

Newman develops this thought in *The Dream of Gerontius*. The soul, having passed the demons, is asking about its present state of separation from the body and says that it was always comforted in life by the thought that it would see God once before going to its purgation. The Angel replies:

> *Yes,—for one moment thou shalt see thy Lord.*
> *. . . that sight of the Most Fair*
> *Will gladden thee, but it will pierce thee too.*
> *[For] the flame of Everlasting Love*
> *Doth burn ere it transform.*

In the evening of life we shall by judged by Love. The angels sing of the soul's approaching agony, an agony which is the sight of Love, as the soul feels both the tremendous attraction and drawing power of Love and, at the same time, is aware of its sin as opposition to Love, as something which simply cannot exist in the actual presence of Love.

> *And these two pains, so counter and so keen,—*
> *The longing for Him, when thou seest Him not;*
> *The shame of self at thought of seeing Him,—*
> *Will be thy veriest, sharpest purgatory.*

Nevertheless the soul is drawn irresistably to the feet of its Lord and darts from the Angel's hold, who can sing of its state:

> *O happy, suffering soul! for it is safe,*
> *Consumed, yet quickened, by the glance of God.*

Purification begins when the soul sees Christ and perceives the mercy of him who said, 'I will have mercy and not sacrifice; for I am not come to call the righteous but sinners to repentance'. (Matt. 9:13) The divine love goes out to meet the acknowledgement of the sinner that every creature belongs to God; but there must be free acceptance of the mercy. Without that free acceptance of mercy there is only the horror of sin and the appallingness of death as it blinds and cripples the soul.

Therefore we must so build up our spiritual life that our whole self would with open eyes perceive the divine mercy in Christ who before his death said, 'I came not to judge the world, but to save the world', and 'I, if I be lifted up from the earth, will draw all men unto me' (John 12:47,32). What is not for God in us can have no place in eternity. All that is not of him must be burnt away so that that which is of him may be carried into the unity. All that is not of him that is not burnt away will go 'to the place ordained for it'.

Conclusion

Our Lord gives us a picture of the Divine Mercy in the parables of the Lost Sheep, the Lost Coin and the Prodigal Son. To each of them the refrain is that 'there is joy among the angels of God over one sinner who repents'. (Luke 15: 10) It is for us so to live in penitence and dependence that we may contribute to this heavenly joy. Our Lord explained to the apostles the necessity of his sacrificial death in order that they could know the joy that none can take away from those who are in Christ (cf. John 16:19-22). It is promised to the faithful servant that he will enter into the joy of the Lord. (Matt. 25:21) St. Paul bids the Thessalonians be comforted and joyful because of the whole continuity of redemption. Because God has acted they can glory. 'For God has not destined us to the terrors of judgement, but to the full attainment of salvation through our Lord Jesus Christ'. Therefore, 'Be always joyful; give thanks whatever happens; for this is what God in Christ wills for you'. (1 Thess. 4:13; 5:18)

It is in the spirit of such joy and with confidence in the triumphant love of God that we can give fulness of content to the words of our prayer:

May the souls of all the departed,
through the mercy of God,
rest in peace.
Amen.